ChapWoman's
GUIDE TO
SHEMANSHIP

and

PILOT HANDLING

by

ANNE LORIMER SIRNA
ANTONIA FERNÁNDEZ RITCHIE

Illustrations by SAM NICHOLS

Seven Seas Press

P.O. Box 220, Rt. 1
Camden, Maine 04843

Dedicated to our husbands,
John and David,
who taught us the way of the wind.

Published by Seven Seas Press/International Marine Publishing Company

10 9 8 7 6 5

Pan American and International Library of Congress Catalog
Card Number: 86-72289

ISBN: 0-915160-93-5

Seven Seas Press/International Marine Publishing Company offers software for sale.
For information and a catalog, please contact TAB Software Department,
Blue Ridge Summit, PA 17294-0850.

Questions regarding the content of this book should be addressed to:

International Marine Publishing Company
Division of TAB Books, Inc.
P.O. Box 220
Camden, ME 04843

Printed by BookCrafters, Inc., Chelsea, MI.
Mechanical Layout & Design by Molly Brown.
Illustrated by Sam Nichols.
Printing Consultants: Karla Fahnestock and Patricia Mullen

Ahoy, Mates:

We decided to write *Chap Woman's Guide to Shemanship and Pilot Handling* when we discovered that the only books written specifically for women afloat are about cooking. Not all women of the sea want to sauté fruited fish, bake beer bread, or charcoal-broil spam bombes.

Some simply want to survive and others want to talk to a sailing wife who tells it like it is—which may be entirely different from the way the Captain tells it. We wish we could invite each of you topside for a mug of coffee, but since we can't, we've written *Shemanship and Pilot Handling* just for you.

Our Guide addresses itself primarily to women who love men who love boats, and women who worry about no longer loving men because they love boats, and women who finally learn to adjust to a "ménage à trois." It also offers a definitive look at life on the open water as seen through the clear, far-sighted eyes of a woman.

This woman is, to put it bluntly, past the first bloom of youth. Chap Woman went to sea under protest, but once she got there, she started paying attention. Her younger counterparts may approach sailing with a different point of view, but we feel that Chap Woman has something to teach them.

When women go to sea, a new set of images and possibilities develop. These may take a while to blossom. But Chap Woman knows there is no reason for any woman to come off as a wimp just because she is confronted with a new situation. After all, she is dealing with Mother Nature and that gives her an elemental understanding of what is going on.

We wonder if you are ambivalent about the boating life. That's the way we began. We've sunned on the foredeck, reading a good book, and been glad we were there. We've worn a safety harness and foul weather gear in a hurricane and vowed to sell the boat if we got home alive.

In our years afloat we have run aground, out of water, and out of patience. But we wouldn't give up the experience.

Yes, sailing is twenty percent peace, twenty percent panic, and sixty percent endurance. After all, spending Friday to Sunday on a sailboat is a lot like spending the weekend on a jungle-gym.

But there is so much more to sailing than that. Out there in the expanse of sea and sky, pounded by wind and waves, the Captain and the mate feel their insignificance in the great palm of nature and their need for one another. In that lonely vastness, we learn our strengths and weaknesses, and in time, come to a competent reckoning with the sea and with ourselves. We discover the meaning of intimacy as we work together side by side to keep our vessel on her true course. Understanding this, we can enjoy each other's idiosyncracies with good humor and laughter.

If you can learn to laugh while you learn to sail, Chap-Woman promises that there will come a time when you will pronounce yourself *Sheworthy*, knowing that on your boat you are confident and competent. You know that boating has truly become part of your life when, with feet planted firmly on terra firma, you find yourself staring wistfully through the chain link fence which separates you from the sea.

We chose ChapWoman to personify the voice of reason and sanity in the midst of mayhem afloat. She represents the female counterpart of the famous Captain Chapman who wrote the definitive book, *Piloting, Seamanship and Small Boat Handling*. ChapWoman will lead you through the intricacies of sailing, guiding you from A to Z, pointing out the shoals and reefs en route.

We hope you enjoy reading *ChapWoman's Guide to Shemanship and Pilot Handling* as much as we've enjoyed writing it. Let us sail with you. We want our book to find a place on your boat, even if it's only in your head.

Anchors Aweigh,

Anne Lorimer Suina
Antonia Fernández Ritchie

Table of Contents

 **is for Anchor**

A is for Anchor. There is one basic rule which Chap-Woman suggests you learn by heart: "Never go anywhere on a boat until you have figured out how to get yourself back to dry land."

Its corollary reads: "An anchor is like the American Express Card. Don't leave home without it."

When the engine fails, the wind dies or night falls, it is comforting to know that the anchor is lying there, up forward, nestled in its coil of rope or chain. It is just waiting to be cast overboard, so that it can dig into the bottom and keep the boat in one particular place for as long as you may wish it to do so.

Keep in mind, however, that down through the ages, the anchor has been the symbol of hope . . . not of faith. Only a landlubber has faith; sailors check the anchor all night long, the way they used to check the kids.

Anchors come in various shapes and sizes and have nautical names like Hereshoff, Danforth, Northill and Bruce. The latter is the "in" anchor at present. New owners are frequently seen standing on the foredeck gazing with pride at their recent acquisition and saying: "Why, yes . . . it's a Bruce." Few ever used that hushed tone of reverence when talking about their newborn sons.

The first step in anchoring is selecting the spot. Usually that spot is closer to the other boats than you want it to be. Your Captain says that he wants to get away from it all, but remember that every man born has the herd instinct. Men clump together, like cattle in the rain, at football games, bars, fitness centers . . . and anchorages. It's something they learned at eighth grade parties. If there is a single boat in an otherwise deserted lagoon, the Captain will sidle right up to it. Whenever possible, ChapWoman suggests setting the anchor a quarter mile from the nearest boat, thus leaving a wide margin for error.

As the Captain puts the boat in reverse, release the anchor line slowly, hand over hand. Lower the anchor gently into the water to prevent chipping, cracking, gouging or fouling. "Foul" is a nautical term sometimes used to describe what happens to the anchor, and sometimes used to describe the Captain's disposition while anchoring. When the Captain asks how much has been payed out, refrain from mention of blood and sweat. Answer him in feet or fathoms.

In the interest of health and harmony while anchoring, make sure that the other end of the anchor line is tied to something solid, and that you are not standing with one foot in the coiled anchor line. Only the anchor should go overboard.

Make yourself as comfortable as possible while waiting to see if the boat is drifting or dragging. Your task is accomplished by taking bearings on several landmarks and then looking for a change in position. This is not easy since your boat and all those boats surrounding you are swinging in big circles at the end of their respective tethers. Everything in your range of vision changes constantly. What doesn't seem to change is that all those boats appear to be getting closer to each other and to you. The Captain assures you that this an illusion due to a windshift and that soon the boats will straighten out and point in the same direction. DO NOT BELIEVE HIM.

When it is time for you to depart, you will discover that the anchor has, at last, understood and accepted the purpose for which it was created. No more slipping and sliding around. No sir. The anchor has found its raison d'être and it is not going anywhere without a struggle. It clings frantically to the bottom, kicking and screaming as you haul it to the surface. It comes aboard under protest, bringing along as much alluvial deposit of mud, sand, shell and oil as it can manage to dump on your freshly scrubbed deck.

This chapter would not be complete without mention of dragging anchor in the middle of the night.

The anchor that has been set and re-set and that has held

You look out of the porthole and see a strange man with nothing on pushing at your boat and hissing to his wife to "Fend Off."

during cocktails and dinner may betray you as the night wears on.

All seems serene as you settle in for sleep in your secluded haven, far from your nearest neighbor. You do not have the faintest premonition of the horror and mayhem to come.

The wind rises. It howls and moans. The Captain is restless. He wakens you every time you fall asleep. He doesn't mean to, it's just that he steps on your head whenever he climbs out of the vee berth to check the anchor. Finally satisfied, he goes to sleep.

But now you're wide awake. You lie there and listen to the pelting rain, convinced the storm has reached gale proportions.

You look out of the porthole and see a strange man with nothing on, pushing at your boat and hissing at his wife to: "Fend Off."

She is calling up to him that she has to put some clothes on if she is to go on deck in the pouring rain. He says that it's night, and that he doesn't have anything on and that nobody will notice. You have already noticed!

So you and the Captain join them on deck. You are going to get to know them very well because your spreaders are locked, your anchor lines are tangled, and your life-lines are twisted. Perhaps you will sail together forever.

The wind is screaming, all hell is breaking loose, and you can't see anything but rain. You fend off, you untangle, you fend off, you untwist. Your teeth chatter. You don't know if its the cold or terror.

The Captain hauls up the anchor and bellows at you: "Take the helm. Don't hit anybody. Don't cut any anchor lines. And, for God's sake, look where you're going."

Suddenly, all sorts of people in foul weather gear appear in the cockpits of their boats. They have heard that you are going to be at the wheel.

ChapWoman understands how dragging anchor may dampen the spirits of even the most ardent boaters.

 **is for Boat Show Fever**

B is for the Boat Show Fever. Boat Show Fever reaches epidemic proportions in the flu season. Usually, it is the male of the species who is affected. However, he may spread the contagion to wife and children. The only known cure is to buy a boat, but this is only temporary because soon the victim must have a bigger boat. And then a bigger one.

ChapWoman has noticed that the earliest symptoms of Boat Show Fever occur in childhood but go undiagnosed for twenty years or more. The afflicted one is the toddler, who heads for the biggest mud puddle on the block. When his friends float milkweed pods in the stream, he puts a toothpick and a bit of bed sheet on his. In math class, he adds a boom and a mast to his isosceles triangles; he thinks the Ancient Mariner had it made.

Soon he's sneaking in a bit of summer Sunfish sailing. He buys a Ted Turner tee shirt and knows that a sextant has nothing to do with sex. He goes to college and meets Someone-Who-Sails-to-Bermuda.

But he also meets a girl and falls in love. Boat Show Fever is in its latent stage. He has a house in the suburbs, two kids and a doorbell with a chime. He mulches flower beds, plants trees, and coaches the Little League. On the surface he is a typical suburbanite who worries about his grass.

But . . . he has a secret subscription to *Sail* delivered in a plain, brown wrapper. He spends long, lingering lunch hours in marine stores fingering braided line and fondling teak trim. He carries shackles in his pocket and buys an oiled wool sweater and a Greek fisherman's hat.

Still, you don't suspect his closet illness until he slips and gives you a fog horn for a burglar alarm and an anchor for a door stop. He checks the compass heading before he goes to work, and says the only problem with the house is that it doesn't go to weather. Then he starts wearing one red and one green sock after dark — "running socks," he says, but he doesn't jog. Next, he is talking port and starboard and soon the baby is teething on cringles.

Finally, on a dreary Saturday in February when you'd do anything to get out of the house, he tells you to put on your sneakers. He's taking you to the city. You are instantly suspicious; the two don't go together. No, you're not going to the museum or to the symphony. You're going to the Boat Show.

It's the beginning of the end. Boats are lying all over the floor of the convention center like great beached whales and he's delirious. The family breadwinner has climbed up a ladder to the deck of a forty foot sloop. He is leaning over the bowsprit muttering, "Land Ho." Well, of course there's land. He's only twenty feet off the floor of the convention center.

And he's speaking a different language. The man whose toothpaste you've been sharing for lo these many years, is jabbering away and you don't understand a word he's saying. Ribs aren't what your son broke on the football field, chine isn't the sound of the grandfather's clock, and line isn't the telephone cord. Scope doesn't mean you ate onions for lunch and sole has nothing to do with fish, your feet or God.

Can this be the man you married? The one who needs a life preserver in the bathtub? He's sitting at something called a chart table, which looks like a desk to you, pompously talking about going offshore. More like off his rocker, you think.

Rather than laugh hysterically, you check out the accommodations. It's a mistake. You'd either be sleeping on something that looks like the ironing board or in the vee berth, which sleeps two if you cut off one set of legs at the knees. Or else you could sleep on the dining room table. Your mother taught you to keep your elbows off the table. One hundred years of civilization swept away in an instant.

Just when you realize that only cold water comes out of the faucet, he says, "Guess what, honey? This one is on

Could this be the man you married — the one who needs a life preserver in the bathtub?

special — only $90,000 sail away price!" Now you're sure he's gone quite mad.

You look beyond the plastic flowers on the table, the velvet throw cushions and the plates with nautical flags. You see the rubber bottoms on those plates and know the awful truth. Obviously, nobody expects this cute, little table to remain steadfast and calm in the rough going ahead. Why should they expect it of you?

This boat has no mast or sails. When it gets them, it will never be dry or flat again. The kids need braces, the house needs a new roof, and he's talking about a $90,000 special! Special to you means two boxes of detergent for the price of one, or getting the kids' turtlenecks marked down from $20 to $8.99.

It's all downhill after that. Boat Show Fever is out in the open. His briefcase bulges with sailing magazines and marine catalogues instead of annual reports. UPS makes weekly deliveries of things you don't need because you don't have a boat. Yet. He holds up his pants with sail ties and wears crossed winches with his dinner clothes.

He's out of control, immune to such common cures as a new set of golf clubs, a business promotion with a year in Europe, or the threat of missing the kids' teenage years—particularly to that one. He'd like to miss them.

He has crossed over the line between chatting about the Chesapeake to talking about buying a boat! So a few boat shows later, he tells you that sailing would be a nice hobby for the two of you, a diversion away from the kids. A way to get a bit of glow back in the marriage. You say you don't think your marriage will do much glowing in a twenty-three foot boat, with a pull out sink, a porta-potty under the bed, and your legs chopped off at the knees. He buys it anyway. He can't stand up in it. He can't sit down too comfortably, either. So, next year he succumbs to another bout of Boat Show Fever.

He mortgages the house—who needs it—and buys a bigger boat with an enclosed head and a fixed galley. He says he's doing it for you. That's what they all say.

In the terminal stages, he keeps "stepping up." Sailors only step down to get into the cabin. First, there's pressurized hot and cold water, an aft cabin, a shower, and a dodger, which has nothing to do with baseball, and finally a ketch with fifteen bags of sails. When the end comes, he sells the house, lives aboard and goes wherever the wind blows.

 **is for Canvas**

C is for Canvas and canvas means sails to an Old Salt. Sails are what make the boat go. Now, don't get ChapWoman wrong, you aren't going to go very fast. In fact, there are many times when you won't go at all. When there isn't any wind and the temperature is 110° and the ice has melted and you'd kill for a cold shower, the sail will hang limply from the mast.

You'll sit dehydrating in the middle of a lake or a bay or an ocean waiting for a puff of breeze or for your Captain to turn on the engine. You'll wait a long time for that. Your Captain is a purist who says things like, "What do you think this is anyway — a power boat?" while you stick to the cockpit cushions, listen to your nose peel and watch the jelly fish prepare to attack.

Your Captain will remind you of the Pilgrims and Columbus and you'll remind him that half the passengers on those voyages died at sea, and that Columbus would certainly have pushed the little starter button if he'd had a choice. In fact, with an engine he'd have discovered America on the first try instead of zigzagging around the world.

You wonder if the kids will have graduated from college by the time you get back, and whether you'll find a shopping center where the house used to be.

And then the wind comes and it takes six hours to cover the same distance that took twenty minutes in the car. If you complain, and of course you will, your Captain will ignore you and give his sail bags an affectionate little pat. Why, he's as crazy over those sails as he used to be over you.

It's time to get to know your competition. First, there are the "working sails" — the jib and the mainsail. Working sails — brought up in the Puritan ethic — sails that rise at seven and get the boat moving. Even the name inspires confidence. What doesn't, is attaching those stalwart blue collar sails to their halyards. The main halyard has criminal tendencies and is handcuffed at night. It is up to you to unlock it and attach it to the head cringle — not an enviable job. One false move and the halyard escapes to the top of the mast where it swings wild and free. The Captain will raise his voice. Your anchorage mates will send their children below. You will be winched up the mast in pursuit of the halyard. When put to the test, ChapWoman has noticed that even the most devoted mother will let her child wash overboard rather than lose the main halyard.

The genoa or "jenny" is called a "light air" sail which non-sailors might translate as a "no air" sail. Or, why go sailing at all if there isn't any breeze? ChapWoman says that's unfair. The jenny does move the boat. The only problem is that you can't see where, because the jenny stretches from foredeck to cockpit and obscures the helmsman's view of the world around her. The tiny plastic window in the sail gives you thirty seconds of sheer terror between seeing a boat and hearing the deck crack in half.

Now, the staysail, mizzen and the blooper are losers. Your Captain will put the staysail up and take it down and put it up again, convinced that he can coax an extra knot of speed out of the boat. It doesn't take much to know that the staysail is utterly useless unless the wind is abeam at twenty knots, a condition that rarely exists. But don't knock the

There's only one place in your house for ten bags of sails. The bedroom, of course.

staysail. It keeps the Captain out of trouble and too busy to check out bikinis with his binoculars.

The mizzen is a ridiculous little pocket-handkerchief of a sail. The Captain calls it an off-wind sail. Nonsense. The mizzen's main function is to shade the cockpit and hold up the useless staysail. And the blooper? Forget about the blooper. The name says it all.

The spinnaker is a different story. Billowing out in front of you in brilliant colors, unattached to boom or stay, it is a sight to behold. It is also a sight to remember when the wind shifts, and the spinnaker falls in the water, or on top of you, or ties you to the mast for eternity.

Be prepared for your Captain to commission a new bag of sails each year. Soon he'll be cuddling in the vee berth with five different jennys, blooper, mizzen, staysail and spinnaker while you sleep alone on the settee.

You think your time will come in November when he decommissions the boat. ChapWoman knows better. There's only one place in your house for ten bags of sails. The bedroom, of course.

 is for Dinghy

D is for Dinghy. Usually a dinghy is treated like a poor relation, acknowledged but not enthused over, kept at a distance from the center of activity and generally undervalued.

Sometimes the dinghy is made the butt of jokes. Often its chief function is merely to ferry the trash and garbage to an appropriate dumping place, and the dog on board to his.

Because of its size, it is frequently given a cute name. You can almost feel its embarrassment as folks exclaim archly, "Our boat is Sea Spray and the dinghy is Spit" or "We named her Wind Flower and the dinghy is Bug." Small wonder the dinghy gets in some licks and chuckles of its own when it has a chance . . . a few hard knocks against a piling, a couple of bobs and weaves in choppy seas . . . just to even up the score.

Most of the time, however, it pouts in silence, pretending to be good, until you attempt to step gingerly aboard. It responds at once, wriggling with delight as it dumps you in the drink. It is still rocking in the water when you surface, and you would swear that the dinghy makes a sound suspiciously like the giggles coming from the amused onlookers on the other boats.

Getting in and out of the dinghy tests the mettle of a true boater. ChapWoman suggests adopting a Groucho Marx slouch. Keep the knees bent and the fanny close to whatever appears to be flat and solid. Move with assurance and pray a lot.

In every boater's life, the inglorious moment occurs, one very dark night, when you and the Captain climb into the dinghy after drinks and dinner ashore, and realize that you have absolutely no idea where you anchored your boat. You row the dinghy back and forth, and back and forth, searching among the darkened hulks. You're positive you've covered every inch of the huge anchorage. Your boat has disappeared—the one you mortgaged your house and your entire future to buy. Perhaps it has been stolen. Perhaps the anchor didn't hold. Perhaps it has floated away and been run over by a freighter. All that money gone.

You will spend eternity, like Charon in his tiny skiff, endlessly rowing this somber, stygian stretch of water in the dark of night. Eventually, of course, you will find your boat. Eventually, too, you will discover the dinghy's true worth. Because, until you learn to walk on water, the dinghy will be your blessed link to shore, shower and sanity.

A dinghy is like a willful child. Whenever you think you have it firmly in tow, you will find that it has wandered off by itself, and vanished from sight. Even though it appears to want to chart its own course, in the dark of night you will feel the dinghy bump up against the stern of your vessel as if to reassure itself of a larger, protective presence.

Dinghies, dogs and children get on well together. They neither know nor care anything about trim, but they all have low centers of gravity, so it doesn't seem to matter. All of them thrive on jostling, rocking, being doused with water, and covered with sand.

The dog on board has a special relationship with the dinghy, his bridge from boat to beach. Unfortunately, these dogs are extremely early risers. At the crack of dawn, Rover is prancing and ready to ride. His demands for "shore leave" are in direct proportion to the size of his Master's hangover and the ungodliness of the hour.

He hops gaily into the dinghy and awaits his Master's appearance with joyous yelps of anticipation. These gradually increase in volume as the Captain lurches on deck in the pre-dawn silence of the sleeping anchorage.

Rover immediately assumes his place in the bow of the dinghy, standing erect and proud, looking like George Washington crossing the Delaware.

The Captain assumes his place at the oars, sitting stooped and lethargic, looking like Rip Van Winkle in the midpoint of his twenty-year nap.

Rover's demands for "Shore Leave" are in direct proportion to the size of his master's hangover and the ungodliness of the hour.

Once ashore, Rover does not complete his mission. Instead, he picks up a scent and disappears into the woods. His Master sits on a stump and wishes for his cozy berth. Rover returns, has a bracing morning swim, and in a burst of camaraderie, attempts to climb onto his Master's lap.

The Captain envisions their return to the vessel. The dog will be wet and sandy. He will shake in the cockpit, he will shake on the foredeck, he will shake in the cabin. The mate will be angry. The thought of the shaking dog and the angry mate are almost more than he can bear at this hour of the morning. Would God, that he could stay on the shore and let the dog row back alone to shake and spray and embrace and slobber.

ChapWoman's advice to the mate: "Never, ever let on to the Captain that you know how to row the dinghy."

 **is for Engine**

E is for Engine. The Captain, a rag man through and through, prides himself on not using the engine. He sails into his anchorage; he sails into his slip; he would like to sail around the world. The iron monster sleeps in its cave behind the companionway steps, silent, neglected, and ignored while the Captain flaunts his canvas.

It's no wonder that the engine snarls and snorts a bit when prodded, while it makes up its mind whether to roar into action and get moving or lie back and wait for further developments. Usually, the engine opts for the latter.

You are the crew member who cares deeply about the engine. It is all that stands between you and the ageless and indifferent sea. You even know how the engine works. There's an intake stroke when the piston goes down, and a compression stroke when the piston goes up, and a power stroke when the piston goes down, and an exhaust stroke when the piston goes up. All of which means that three quarters of a four-stroke cycle engine are useless. The power stroke is the only one worth anything.

Whenever you get involved with engines, you have to think about batteries. The two go together, like the which-came-first-the-chicken-or-the-egg problem. You need the battery to start the engine, and you need the engine to charge the battery.

So why does the Captain scream and tear his hair about running down the battery, when he is always loath to turn on the engine?

When you need the engine, not one of those fifteen bags of sails will take its place. You are somewhere in the middle of nowhere when the wind dies. You can either bob up and down, getting seasick and watching the sharks circle while you run out of water, or you can turn on the engine and motor to land. You are out in a gale when the mainsail tears to shreds. You can either pitchpole, broach, and eventually sink, or you can turn on the engine.

The Captain does not like to turn on the engine, but you have noticed (although you are smart enough not to mention it) that when he finally decides it is time to do so, he's just as anxious as you are for it to start.

Which, of course, is when it refuses. Wondering if the engine will kick over is like waiting for the other shoe to drop. But there's more to starting the engine than pushing the button. You must turn on the blower to get the gasoline fumes out of the bilge so you don't blow up if the engine obliges.

You hang over the stern like a blood-hound, sniffing for fumes. If you don't smell gasoline, you press the starter. It has occurred to ChapWoman that when blowing up is the payoff, you should use something a little more scientific than your nose.

When you begin to think along these lines, there's also the problem of carbon monoxide poisoning. If gasoline fumes collect in the bilge because of inadequate ventilation, so can the exhaust fumes from a running engine. ChapWoman urges you to open a port or a hatch to keep the air moving in the cabin.

Whether or not the Captain likes to use the engine, you can be sure that he will designate one glorious spring weekend to take it apart. Your boat will look like the corner gas station except that the foul, filthy, black motor oil will be in a plastic milk carton on your teak-and-holly sole instead of on a cement floor in a garage, which is where foul, filthy motor oil belongs.

In fact, the entire cabin floor will be littered with piles of tools, oil, pliers, funnels, tubing, WD40 to make the bolts turn, and a suction pump. The engine is diapered in Pampers® in case of oozing engine oil.

The atmosphere is tense. The Captain is about to operate and you are the surgical nurse standing at attention, ready to slap various instruments into his outstretched palm. There's the quarter-inch wrench, the half-inch wrench

The Captain does not like to turn on the engine.

and finally, the inch-and-a-half wrench. God forbid you mix up your inches.

Your one and only is a peculiar sight. His head is somewhere inside the engine and his body is curled in the quarterberth like a giant pretzel. He has removed the quarterberth cushion and the side of the quarterberth next to the engine along with the companionway steps and all the drawers in the galley. At this moment, like a rat on a sinking ship, you are trapped below decks with no escape route.

The Captain is using a hand pump to suction hot, dirty oil into a tube that runs from where he is to where you are. The object of this exercise is to let the oil drip into the plastic milk carton you had been using for drinking water. You know that your Captain is issuing instructions but you can't hear what they are because his voice is muffled by the Pampers®. You do hear him slurping up the oil and know that it is moving inexorably on its way towards you.

It is at times like this that you think maybe the Captain is right and you shouldn't have an engine at all. Then you remember that it is the engine that heats the water for your shower, which you will certainly be needing after you clean up this awful mess.

 is for Freighter

F is for Freighter. In boating, as in life, there is always something looming on the horizon — vast, dark and threatening. Whether or not you can see a freighter, rest assured that it's out there—waiting to get you.

ChapWoman advises you to keep a sharp eye out for freighters, tankers and steamers. Report them as soon as you sight them and keep on reporting them until they have passed you and are at least fifty miles away. Never relax your vigilance on a boat.

Freighters, tankers and steamers appear to be incredibly large and, from a distance, seem to be moving at a snail's pace. This is a misconception. They are not incredibly large . . . they are positively humongous . . . and for something that big, they are zipping along like the Concorde. On sighting a freighter in the distance, your first impression is that there's a brand new island out in the water and, what's more, they built the Trump Tower on it.

Before you can say "Constant Bearing," one of those beauties will be climbing up your transom and blasting you out of its way with a sound that drowns out the screams of the crew.

It's even worse at night. In the dark, when the freighter's lights disappear, it may be because the freighter is directly overhead. When this occurs, you wish you hadn't read *Shipkiller* or *Overboard*. Most mates have read them. They quote from them regularly.

There is one thing to be said for freighters, tankers and steamers: they know their place. What's more, they stay in it, too. It's the "Large Ship Lane" marked in pale green on the charts. Your problem is that the Captain keeps forgetting *his* place. He wants to mosey out there and play with the Big Boys. You remind him that his presence will irritate them, that he will be underfoot, and that one slap from their bow

Before you can say "Constant Bearing," one of those beauties will be climbing up your transom and blasting you out of its way with a sound that drowns out the screams of the crew.

wave could flatten him. You remind him that the best view of a freighter is from abaft the beam. Why can't he just stay on his side of the pale green section like it was the Berlin Wall, or the thirty-eighth parallel, or something?

But, no, boys will be boys and the Captain ignores all your good advice and goes running out into the middle of things. He will give the flimsy excuse that your destination is on the other side of the shipping lane.

You know that when you get out there the wind will die. It does. You sit, becalmed, watching the Trump Tower bearing down on you. You urge the Captain to start the engine and get the hell out of the way. He takes his own good time reaching for the button. The odds of the engine starting on the first try are slim, at best. ChapWoman would remind you that engines rarely start in shipping lanes and hurricanes. They are foolproof only on breezy days, when you don't need them.

Finally, the engine comes to life with seconds to spare. You look up with awe at the sheer face of the great, gray mountain as it slides past. A few people stand atop the behemoth, like tiny figures on a wedding cake. They stare down at you and wave, oblivious of your need for a Coronary Care Unit.

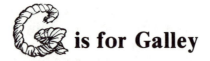# is for Galley

G is for Galley. The results of a recent survey, entitled "How Green Was My Galley" by ChapWoman, prove that most women believe a properly equipped boat would contain a head, but no galley. This, they stated unequivocally, would preclude the vessel's getting too far from shore for too long a stretch. When the carry-on ice chest runs out of food, ninety-eight percent agreed that it's time to head for a restaurant on shore, and a full course meal on a table that doesn't have a raised border running around its edge. The other two percent sided with the Captain, but they're the smart-assed ones who know how to light the alcohol stove without assistance, so their vote didn't count.

The galley consists of two parts—the alcohol stove and the ice box. Now, it seems to ChapWoman that any product whose operating manual begins . . . "Fill a large pot with water in case of fire" . . . is a product to be avoided. And it is by the Captain.

Approach the whole operation of lighting the alcohol stove with caution, because what starts as a small puddle of liquid at the base of the stove will, in thirty seconds, resemble the *Burning of Atlanta*.

Before attempting to light the stove, you must follow these steps:

1) Pump up the pressure in the tank under the stove to get the alcohol to flow. The pump in question has about the same capacity as a small hypodermic syringe and the tank holds about five gallons. Put simply, that means a lot of pumping, honey.

2) Turn on the stove. Contrary to any other kitchen range known to the civilized world, the alcohol stove's dials turn to the left for on; to the right for off. This brings ChapWoman to a basic principle: *Everthing aboard a boat is counter instinctual*. It's important to remember this

precept . . . particularly in moments of stress which occur with amazing frequency in the galley.

3) Peer down the tiny hole beneath the burner while looking for the trickle of alcohol collecting at its base. Try to see it sometime before you feel it dripping on your topsiders.

4) Now light your match and as the flame sears your fingers, reach down that three-and-a half inch deep hole and try to ignite the alcohol lying there.

5) Step back and watch the burner, stove, and galley burst into a magnificent conflagration of purple and gold flame.

6) When the fire dies down, the anticipated moment has arrived. With trembling, charred fingers, strike another match and light the stove. If all has gone well and your timing has been absolutely perfect . . . it *may* work. (Otherwise, pick another burner and start all over again.)

Forty-five minutes later, when the water for one, lousy cup of coffee hasn't come to a boil yet, you may decide to open the ice box and have a cold beer instead.

The ice box may be defined as a deep, dank hole which is filled periodically with blocks of frozen water. These immediately revert to their natural state, which propagates all manner of green things. These multiply with great rapidity.

The ice box is not a pretty place, and the cook would be advised to get in and out of it as quickly as possible. This is difficult because the desired items of food are rarely the ones which keep floating to the surface, through the flotsam and debris.

A single look at the location of the ice box and you'll know the best kept secret of boating . . . Naval architects don't cook.

They have carefully placed the ice box in one of two places. Either it snuggles right beside the engine where it absorbs all the heat of a day's motoring, or it is mounted just where everyone steps below into the cabin. Using the top of

A single look at the location of the ice box and you'll know the best kept secret in boating . . . naval architects don't cook.

the ice box is okay if the lid happens to be in place and the cook is not using the surface to make sandwiches. However, if the lid is not in place, that first step can lead to vast discomfort and is how the expression "getting cold feet" began.

No discussion of the ice box is complete without a few words about the implement used in conjunction with it—the ice pick. This lethal instrument is designed to make chips off the old block. Instead, it is driven with unerring instinct to puncture the sides of any metal container within its range. It shows a special affinity for the aluminum in beer, coke and ginger ale cans. With the boat underway, endeavoring to fill a glass with enough ice for a drink can lead to a display rivaling the *Fountains of Versailles*.

H is for Heel and the Head

H is for the Heel and the Head. Understanding these two basic topics is of the utmost importance for your survival and welfare aboard ship.

Let us start with the Heel. You must remember at all times that when a sailboat is doing what it is designed to do — that is, sail — it is not a very relaxing place to be. The only difference between a sailboat's cabin while the vessel is underway and the tilted room of a funhouse, is that the angle of incline of the sailboat is appreciably greater.

If you think the Olympic gymnasts were spectacular, just wait till you try grabbing for the overhead handholds in the cabin while making six-and-a half knots under sail.

The Head . . . the only part of the anatomy that could possibly fit into the space allotted.

What ChapWoman means is, if it isn't nailed down, it's going to slide. This applies to every item on the vessel, including the Captain and you.

In nautical terms, this phenomenon is referred to as the Heel, and is due to the force of the apparent wind on the sails, producing the lateral pressure which, in turn, is counterbalanced by the lateral resistance of the hull and its righting moment.

It may also be defined as the boat rolling over on its side and playing dead in spite of your earnest exhortations to the Captain to "straighten this damn thing up!"

While you are frantically clutching for the high side of the boat, while you listen to the sound of breaking glass (which is probably the gin bottle or the binoculars, which you now remember you left on the counter, instead of putting in the locker), while your toes are turning purple from being curled in panic inside your brand new boat shoes, while you are practicing your primal scream . . . the Captain, completely unaware that anything is amiss, may announce casually that it would be nice if you went below and got him a beer. It's about now that the word "Heel" becomes a more apt description of your former bed-mate, whom you'll be seeing a lawyer about as soon as you get back to dry land.

Now, let us turn our attention to the Head, which is what the toilet area is called in boating parlance . . . probably because that is the only part of the anatomy that could possibly fit into the space allotted. If you are unfamiliar with the Head, you might practice backing into your broom closet at home to get the feel of things.

The Head is a strange and wonderful arrangement. It is operated by a series of complicated valves and pumps. Ask advice *before* using the facilities, since one false move may flood the entire cabin (and not only with epithets from the Captain!).

Sometimes the Head is surrounded on three sides by walls or curtains. Often it sits smack in the center of the cabin, alone in its glory by day. But not at night. When those assigned to sleep up forward go to bed, they may take the Head with them. It's now located *under* their vee-berth snugly secure for the night. The Captain tells you that space is essential aboard a boat. You whimper that it's also essential to your bladder. Nobody cares.

Mastery of the Heel and the Head is acquired with time and practice, but it also helps to have one leg ten inches longer than the other and the kidneys of a camel.

I is for Inner Ear

I is for Inner Ear. You may wonder why you need to read about your inner ear in a sailing primer. The answer, quite simply, is that the inner ear controls motion sickness and no book about sailing would be complete without a chapter on throwing up.

Now don't get ChapWoman wrong. There will be many blissful times in your boating career when the sea or river or ocean of your choice is flat. The Captain may complain but you and your stomach will lie peacefully on deck, catching the rays and contemplating the meaning of life.

You won't even know that your stomach is there curled up between liver and pancreas, quietly digesting lunch. It seems reasonable always to sail under these conditions.

Alas, your Captain is not a reasonable man. There is a bit of Ahab, Bligh and Queeg in most men of the sea. So . . . when the bay turns mean and the ocean sends eight foot rollers booming to shore, when the watermen stay safely in their slips because the Coast Guard has issued small craft warnings, your Captain will decide to set sail to see how bad it really is.

If you are already out there when the bay whips itself into a frenzy and Scylla and Charybdis lurk in the trough of every wave, instead of getting out of the blow, your Captain will announce that he is staying on course because he has already paid for a slip at the Baltimore Inner Harbor.

Your pitiful craft climbs, crashes and lurches over every wave, rolls sideways, pitches, sways, climbs, crashes and rolls some more. And some more and some more.

Your stomach does the same thing. It has become a separate entity, tossing about behind your waist, slapping against your ribs, turning somersaults and cartwheels, crying mayday and trying to get off the boat.

In other words you are sick. You never remember being this sick before in your life. You are also turning a hideous shade of green, more bilious looking than a child's tube of monster blood. You try to fix your gaze on something that isn't moving. There isn't anything. Even the compass is floating in oil. You want your mother. You want your bed. You want to pull the covers over your head and die. You want last rites.

It is then that you understand the real problem. Nobody ever dies from being seasick. You will go on living and suffering and being sick and hanging over the rail on the side where the wind is not. The reality, too horrible to contemplate, is knowing that you are four hours from Baltimore.

Your Captain is sympathetic. After all, he doesn't want to clean the boat any more than is necessary. He tells you that you will feel better if you eat something. You don't believe him but you try it anyway. Then he tells you to keep busy. You can't imagine how you will keep busy when your body is frozen in fright and the Captain has to pry your fingers loose from the winch, one at a time, whenever he comes about.

According to your Captain, seasickness is not in your stomach at all but in your inner ear. Considering the way your stomach feels, that is an unlikely story. "Keep your head still and you'll feel just fine," he says, so you cling to the

It really doesn't matter whether you're going to Block Island, the Dry Tortugas or Bermuda, you can look forward to throwing up for part of the trip.

winch and hold your head rigid while the rest of you rolls and topples to port and starboard.

It really doesn't matter whether you're going to Block Island, the Dry Tortugas or Bermuda; you can look forward to throwing up for part of the trip. So it's not surprising that sailors have devised a number of seasick remedies. Some nibble on crackers at sea, while others suck on lemons or hard candy. They swear by full stomachs or by empty ones and take potions or pills or something that bomber pilots used in the Second World War. They sniff spirits of ammonia, count backwards from one thousand in sevens and put camphor in their belly buttons. All the remedies have one thing in common. They don't work.

What does work is the "patch" — a drop of medication on a tab placed behind the ear. There's that inner ear again. You may become sleepy or talkative, telling your cruising mates, whom you only just met, things you wouldn't tell your best friend. Your speech may slur, your eyeballs dilate, your vision blur, but you won't be sick. That's all that counts.

Now the "patch" comes with a warning. You may become disoriented and even hallucinate. But what's a little psychosis compared to being seasick?

 **is for Jibe**

J is for Jibe. When the Captain shouts: "Stand by to Jibe," the wise mate moves instinctively. If you are on deck, fall to your knees as if an apparition has just appeared. If you are in your berth, pull the covers over your head and assume the fetal position. Jibing is dangerous. Don't distract or mess around with the Captain when he is about to jibe. He needs to focus his attention on what he is doing.

There are two kinds of jibe: intentional . . . which is bad enough . . . and unintentional . . . which is absolute murder and may be summed up as: surprise, surprise, you just tore your mainsail to shreds, ripped out all your rigging, sent two people sprawling flat-out unconscious on deck, and dumped a third person overboard.

Jibing consists of bringing the stern of the vessel through the eye of the wind. On a breezy day, when this happens accidentally, the mainsail and the boom career from one side of the boat to the other, sweeping everything before them with a monstrous whoosh.

A jibe also means to utter taunting words. ChapWoman counsels that this is never, ever done on a sailboat after an unintentional jibe . . . angry words, perhaps, hysterical even . . . but never taunting.

The problem with jibing is that is happens when everyone least expects it. There you are, stretched out in the cockpit, luxuriating in the sun, sailing down the bay, wing and wing. You think the brisk, shifting breeze has died. Now, all is calm and peaceful. You are wrong, wrong, wrong. The breeze has not gone away, it's behind you, traveling with you, so you don't feel it anymore.

As you enjoy the peace and quiet, the wind gradually sneaks around behind the mainsail. (Perhaps the helmsman got a teeny, weeny bit off course.) Now you're not moving with the wind anymore and the alert mate may notice a faint

When the Captain shouts: "Stand by to Jibe," the wise mate moves instinctively.

stirring of breeze under the boom. It is time to advise the helmsman that he is sailing by the lee. In real life, you shout: "Look out!" The Captain says: "Why?" and the boom slashes across the deck, wiping out all before it.

The only way to avoid this sort of mayhem is to keep a sharp eye on the wind and know what it is doing. (This is the same sharp eye that you always have peeled for freighters, tankers, and steamers out there.) ChapWoman knows it is difficult to keep track of the wind which is invisible as well as shifty . . . but nobody ever said sailing was easy.

Since you can't see the wind, one way to be aware of what it is up to is to watch your tell-tales. Tell-tales are wind direction indicators that are tied to—you'll never believe this one—the . . . shrouds. Shrouds are wires that keep the mast from falling over sideways.

Tell-tales are just about the best bargain in boating. It's a wise mate who saves her yarn scraps and needlepoint threads all winter long to tie onto her shrouds come the sailing season. Hair ribbons are good and old cassette tapes make excellent tell-tales.

There is one other item that should be mentioned in connection with jibing. Namely, the preventer — a line tied to the boom and then fastened to a cleat up forward on the deck. It's a bit like putting a muzzle and chain on a troublesome dog. With the preventer in place, the mate can relax her vigil, knowing that for the time being, the boom is not going anywhere dangerous, nor will it snap out at innocent bystanders.

If only she could find a way to fasten a preventer to the Captain.

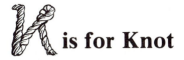 **is for Knot**

K is for Knot, which is something a sailor likes to tie in the lengths of line he has squirreled away throughout his vessel.

Like his bushy-tailed counterpart, the Captain never feels he has enough to last him through the trying times ahead. Bright-eyed and busy, he has filled the anchor locker in the peak, the lazarette in the stern, and all the spaces in between with lengths and lengths of line. Still, the Captain keeps adding more: nylon, dacron, polypropylene, and even a little old fashioned hemp are placed with the piles he has stashed away.

Line is a general term applied to a piece of rope in use. You make fast with a line, but you trim a sail with a sheet. Actually, there are only nine ropes on a boat: bell, man, top, foot, bolt, back, yard, bucket and tiller. The latter information may help you in trivia games but it doesn't seem to come up much on a sailboat.

The mate understands that line, with a knot on the end, is what attaches the boat to things that don't move, like land, the bottom of the bay, an already anchored boat, or, best of all, to each one of the pilings on the four corners of your slip in the marina.

So ChapWoman recommends knowing your Knots. The mate who can tie a bowline with confidence is one who can face approaching a dock in gale winds with resolute courage. No double overhand panic knots on her pilings.

The bowline has a lot going for it. It won't jam and is easy to untie. Use it whenever you want a loop that stays the same size. A fellow sailor will understandingly nod approval and may even join in with you as you chant this nautical ditty as you work: "The rabbit comes out of the hole, goes around the tree, looks about, doesn't like what he sees and goes back into the hole."

Still the Captain keeps adding more.

The figure eight knot doesn't tie anything to anything; it ties itself to itself. Use it at the end of a sheet to keep it from going where it doesn't belong, like up the mast where you-know-who will have to go up after it.

The monkey-fist is a big round ball tied by sailors who want to look like old salts. They use it as a weight on the end of a line they are throwing to somebody, or on the end of their key chains. Monkey-fist key chains are carried by people who wear navy blue blazers, anchors and lighthouses on their neckties and thick soled boat shoes when they attend cocktail parties in southwest Iowa.

The square knot is just like the one you tie on your shoes. Put the line in your right hand over the one in your left hand, and pull them tight. Then put the line now in your left hand over the one in your right, and pull. Do it backwards and you have a granny knot. Grannies got their name because they have the tendency to ease up a little when the going gets rough. Square knots prefer to hold firm and not give an inch.

Two half hitches are used to make a line fast to a piling. Don't be misled into thinking that if two are good, six must be better. Keep it simple, because sooner or later, you'll be the one who has to untie the whole mess. Remember the Posiedon Precept: The line that you want to fasten comes free, the line that you want to slide free catches on everything.

Knot also means the speed of one nautical mile (6080 feet) per hour. Remember a knot is not a measure of distance but a rate of speed. ChapWoman warns that this rate of speed is knot very fast. Knot at all. Actually, you could make far better time pedaling a bicycle.

The Captain likes to use the phrase 60 D STreet. By that, he means the speed times the time equals the distance times sixty.

Most cruising sailboats manage, at best, a top speed of six or seven knots; most cruising sailboat captains plan a day's journey of thirty-five or forty nautical miles. Most cruising mates do some mental arithmetic and fall back into their berths groaning in disbelief.

The problem here lies in the fact that the Captain always uses the boat's top speed in his calculations. The mate understands that the vessel actually hit this top speed once, for twenty-five seconds one afternoon, two years ago. The words "average speed" don't seem to enter into the Captain's vocabulary and certainly not into his calculations of 60 D STreet.

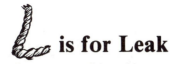 is for Leak

L is for Leak. ChapWoman defines leak as any water in the cabin that doesn't belong there. That includes the rollers that break in the vee berth because somebody left the hatch open; the slosh from the head when the boat heels; the overflow from the water tanks that occurred this morning when you forgot you had the hose running and went back to the car for the groceries; and the cloud burst that drenches the vee berth because somebody left the hatch open, again.

Certainly your craft will look snug and secure swaddled in shrink wrap or covered with canvas in the yard. You may wonder why you spent so much time wrapping it up for the winter when it's going to leak like a sieve for the summer.

Water will dribble down the bulkhead, trickle down the mast and drip into the lockers. All of the portholes will weep. The clothing you brought for a ten-day cruise will be damp from the first afternoon's thunderstorm. It may not be nautically correct, but ChapWoman suggests drying your lingerie on the flag halyard.

Eventually the Captain decrees a lay day to look for leaks. Usually a lay day is your reward—the carrot on the boating stick—a day spent ashore on terra firma. You eat out, browse in shops and buy a newspaper to see if the world is still there. You even shop in the Acme and enjoy it. A lay-over day in port is fun. What the Captain has in mind is anything but.

It's not so bad in the beginning. You stand in the sun with the hose, spraying everything in sight, the way you did as a kid—the chain plates and stanchions, dorades and mast boot. You even spray the Captain when he isn't looking.

But then, when he announces that the port stanchion is leaking, look out. ChapWoman cautions that removing a stanchion (the post that holds up the lifeline) and rebedding it in sealant, strains the most loving relationship.

Eventually, the Captain decrees a day to look for leaks.

The Captain stands on deck, gripping the stanchion base. You lie belly up on the settee, reaching inside the locker with a socket wrench to which the Captain has added an extension and a swivel joint. A six foot arm would make your job easier.

You are trying to remove the four bolts that hold the stanchion, but you can't see what you are doing. You can only hope that you are not unbolting the deck from the hull. In the dark one bolt feels pretty much like another. The Captain is banging on the deck above your left ear. He has decided that you *are* unbolting the deck.

You lie there staring into the darkness, wrestling with the problem. If a right hand screw advances when you turn it clockwise, and you are now looking at it upside down—that is, if you could see it—does the nut holding the bolt turn to the left? You wonder if the nautical maxim, "Righty tighty, lefty loosey" holds true here.

Once the stanchion has been rebedded, the Captain feels the thrill of victory. "We got it this time—once and for all," he crows. He is into guerilla warfare. He hoses the boat again, dousing the stanchion. You sit below and watch the water trickle down the bulkhead. He's been ambushed.

The leaks have a hideout the Captain can't penetrate—the hollow cavity between the inner and outer skin of the cabin top. Water that appears to drip from the stanchion started somewhere else.

You may learn to adapt to the splash of water below decks, but few mates are willing to accept the geyser that spouts from the cabin sole every time the Captain decides to remove a through hull fitting to clean the knot meter. This is not a leak, it's a sinking.

The Captain starts taking the boat apart when he is bored. He abandons you at the helm in the middle of a regatta. There you are with forty two spinnakers headed straight at you. The Captain is on his knees with Old Faithful gushing up in the cabin. Also, it looks suspiciously like your toothbrush he's using to clean the sludge, slime and seaweed off the knot meter.

Common sense tells you that there is no reason good enough to justify pulling the plug out of a boat that is sitting in the water. You mention to him as you have before and will again that a woman would never have designed a boat this way. And that he'd better use his own toothbrush next time.

While the Captain wages war against leaks, you are engaged in hand to hand combat with mildew. You scrub it; you hang bags of crystals from the hand rails and set out pots of crystals on the counters. You get out the heavy artillery and install fancy vents that suck out the stale air. You plug in gadgets that heat moist air. But as soon as your back is turned, the mildew advances, pushing forward across the quarterberth, and marching up the bulkhead. The head is under siege. You will never surrender, but you can't win either.

In the war against leaks, there is no victory at sea. ChapWoman advises that the best you can expect is an armed truce.

 **is for Mutiny**

M is for Mutiny. ChapWoman abhors violence but agrees that desperate times call for desperate measures. There is always more than one way to weather the storm and keep one's head above water. A mutinous mate has a lot more power than she realizes. The Captain needs two hands to get where he is going, and those hands are at the end of your arms.

You may use them cooperatively if he will agree to head for shore when gloom and doom strike, or you may practice passive resistance by sitting on them and refusing to take the helm if he won't. If the Captain turns a deaf ear to the voice of reason, say nothing further, but adopt aggressive action. Begin by throwing all the food overboard. Move on to the liquor. The Captain will come to his senses.

Certainly, there are many times at sea when you must put up and shut up; but there are other times when Chap-Woman feels it is quite acceptable to mutiny. Here are some of them:

1) After seven days at sea, you make landfall and come into port for provisions. You see other humans. It is a time to dance, shout, eat out. The Captain has other plans. He liked the solitude. He hates crowds. He announces that he wants to anchor in peace and eat aboard. ChapWoman says: jump ship. Immediately.

2) The wind is gusting to forty knots. The Naval Academy just cancelled its race because of the safety factor. You, of course, are out there in the blow. The tiller snaps. Your boat tumbles and rolls while the Captain tries to jury-rig a steering device. You spot a Coast Guard vessel and start to summon assistance. The Captain stops you. "They are going to help a boat in distress. Don't interrupt them," he says. If your craft is smashed to bits on Sparrows Point, remember, at least it's land. Hitchhike home. Without a backward glance.

He tells you that his immediate future plans include some offshore sailing. Sell your half of the boat immediately.

3) The Captain is into conserving his batteries. You cook dinner for six by the light from the alcohol stove, and set the table from the glow of the flickering bug candle. It's not easy, but you do it. Then the Captain insists that he must inspect the bilge before anyone eats. Access to the bilge involves disturbing your dinner, dismantling your table, disrupting your guests. Throw the Captain's steak overboard.

4) The temperature is 101°. There is no wind. You petition the Captain to turn on the engine to get you where you are going, which is either an air-conditioned restaurant or the marina pool. He wants to continue drifting among the giant green-heads on his cruise to nowhere. He scoffs at your request to break out the iron-jib. Cut the dinghy loose and flag down the nearest passing vessel. Request a tow to shore.

5) You tell the Captain he is going to run aground. You know this because he ran aground on this spot last year. He ignores you. He runs hard aground, harder still as he tries to escape. When he asks you why you didn't warn him about the thin water, remain silent. As far as you are concerned, your only activity aboard ship will be listening to the ice melt and the food spoil. Don't sail again until the Fall.

6) The Captain considers the cruise itinerary his bible. Thou shalt make each anchorage on schedule. Honor thy destination. Thou shalt ignore all gale warnings. Remember thou keep holy thy E.T.A. So you set sail into the midst of the hurricane, and are blown across the bay with the boat half under water. Once at the designated anchorage, you find you are alone. The rest of the group stayed put in Annapolis and are having a ball in town. Have a large belt yourself then dump the liquor overboard.

7) You want new boat upholstery because what you have now is patched with duct tape. The sponge rubber in the cushions has the resiliency of wilted lettuce leaves. The Captain wants a Loran. He considers upholstery irrelevant. You wonder why he needs Loran to gunkhole in the Chesapeake Bay. He tells you that his immediate future plans include some offshore sailing. Sell your half of the boat immediately.

 is for Navigation

N is for Navigation. ChapWoman defines Navigation as any means used to get a boat from one place to another.

On small sailboats, this usually requires the use of the tiller. Always push it in the opposite direction from the way you want to go. Push to the right to go left. Remember: everything aboard a boat is counter-instinctual.

A Captain who was anxious to avoid having his crew run the boat aground again, devised this method to practice steering at home. Take your child's red wagon to the top of a steep incline, turn it around and sit in it with the handle behind you and coast down the hill. With repeated practice, you'll get the hang of managing a tiller. Of course, your child may never forgive you for the damage done his favorite toy, and the neighbors may start some ugly rumors about you.

As soon as you have mastered the tiller, the Captain will trade up to a vessel with a wheel. So now you will have to forget what you have learned, and start over again, this time pretending you are behind the wheel of a car . . . make that a very expensive recreational vehicle . . . and one that doesn't come equipped with brakes.

As the size of the vessel increases, so does the Captain's urge to get further from shore. Charts appear. The Captain starts drawing lines all over them and muttering a lot. You try not to listen. When you do, you hear things like running fix, danger bearing and dead reckoning. It's that last one that shakes the confidence of the crew.

Gone are the carefree days when you simply hoisted the sail and went wherever the wind blew. Now it's a plotted course and steering the boat involves the use of the compass. This is because the Captain, who's busy playing Navigator down in the cabin in the shade, keeps deciding to change the course.

Take your child's red wagon — turn it around and sit in it with the handle behind you and coast down the hill.

You, who are standing at the helm in the blazing sun, try to accommodate him. The compass does not choose to cooperate. Every time you take your eye off it and the compass swerves wildly, the Captain says, "You're not paying attention." You have noticed when the Captain is helmsman and the compass swerves wildly, it's called "windshift."

Meanwhile, the compass sits there in its little binnacle and acts smug. Here is a helpful hint from ChapWoman: just keep looking at the course number and chase it. If it shifts to one side of the line, turn the wheel after it; when it shifts to the other side, turn the wheel to that side. Your boat will waddle down the bay, but you'll be on course.

Each cruising morning, you will find your Captain hunched over his charts, making pencil marks on them that closely resemble runic characters. He uses dots and squiggles, squares and half circles. He throws in a few arcs and several angles. He connects all of these with straight lines. He erases a lot. Then he announces importantly that he has plotted today's course. He has included vectors for set and drift. He has his pelorus at the ready. It will be a busy day.

Meanwhile, ChapWoman suggests that you stall around for awhile in the anchorage until you spot a boat leaving ahead of you which seems to be going to the right direction. Follow it.

No chapter on navigation would be complete without mention of the words: "Celestial Navigation." Okay. They have been mentioned. ChapWoman understands that you certainly will never, ever get yourself into the position where you will need to use the stars to find your way home. It would mean that you were either lost at sea or, God forbid, racing to Bermuda.

 **is for Offshore**

O is for Offshore. ChapWoman has noticed that there is a moment in every Captain's life when he decides that This Is the Summer to Go Offshore. It is also the summer you have been dreading ever since he bought the boat. It's okay with you if he wants to get into the lonely sea and the running tide bit but it's not okay that he wants to take you with him.

You're into boundaries and edges, four hour sails and dinner in Annapolis. And an anchor. Particularly an anchor with those nice yellow tabs on the rode. None of this hundred fathoms deep stuff for you.

Doesn't he know that there are sharks, the Bermuda Triangle and Russian subs offshore? So you buy him "Forty Days on a Life Raft" to make your point and he buys you a light for your PFD to make his. When you're bobbing around alone in the ocean, you'll be able to see what's going to get you before it does.

Finally, he brings home an inflatable life raft and blows it up in the living room. You are going to sea like Ulysses. You wish you didn't remember how long it took him to get home again. Anyway, you climb into the raft along with the dogs and the kids. It's sort of cozy in a life raft in front of the fireplace. But that's not where you'll be using it.

So you begin to get your life in order as you prepare for the end. You clean out the bureau drawers, send a birthday card to your mother six months early, balance your checkbook, leave lists for your descendents and arrange for snow removal. You want to be remembered as One Who Did Her Job.

Your Captain wants to be remembered as an intrepid explorer who took a thirty foot boat one hundred miles offshore, out of all radio contact with land—out where the Russian trawlers play. This is the first time that you realize that your father was right all along. Opposites may attract but they should never marry.

Your boat is no happier about going offshore than you are. The Captain has taken it out of its nice, cozy slip and abandoned it on a mooring near the ocean. There it lies the night of departure, thrashing about wildly, trying to get away from the roar of the waves crashing right outside the breakwater.

The boat knows more than the Captain about what lies ahead. You remind him that Bermuda was discovered in the early 16th century and then lost again for one hundred years. The same could happen to you. But he isn't the least bit concerned.

So you cast off and for a time all goes well. That first evening may lull you into believing that this isn't going to be so bad after all. The sun sets and you see the lights of the shore. You are not alone. As darkness falls and the stars twinkle and you sail in the shimmering moon path, you may even think that it is nice out there.

Pay no attention to these thoughts. It is not nice out there. The Captain will wake you at 3:00 a.m., exactly five minutes after you have finally fallen asleep, to tell you that it is time for your watch. He wants the bed. It is then that you know the truth. It is terrible out there. Nobody told you that the boat would be soaking wet. There are no boats, no lights, and even the stars and moon are gone. Maybe the rest of the world knows something that your Captain doesn't, like there is about to be a nuclear attack. After all, the radio doesn't work one hundred miles offshore.

The only sound is the whoosh and swoosh of the waves and your watchmate throwing up. You'll never complain about the noise of the TV and the stereo again, if you get out of this alive.

If this is to be your first trip offshore, you need to know that life offshore consists of four basic elements. These are food, sleep, standing watch and trying not to go below to use the head.

Doesn't he know that there are sharks, the Bermuda Triangle and Russian subs offshore?

Your boat may sleep six but all you will use are the settees in the main cabin. There is no such thing as offshore sex. The vee-berth will be bucking from Cape May to New England and the quarterberth will be full of beer.

You lie on the settee like a mummy in a tomb, held in place by a lee cloth that reminds you of a shroud. You wish it didn't. At least it separates you from all the gear that is banging about the cabin sole. It's not a comfortable place to be, but you won't be there very long. No, you will be standing watch three hours on and three hours off all day and all night.

The first time that you do it, you think that standing watch is another one of those nautical terms that doesn't mean very much. What you are watching is the bow of the boat and your watchmate huddled in a sick ball in the corner of the cockpit trying to keep dry and warm.

By the second night out, however, when you struggle below after your watch is completed, you are wet, cold, tired and exultant. Tonight, you have kept the right star in the spreader and the boat on her course. This afternoon, you survived a storm at sea.

When a howling wind whipped the tops off ten foot waves and the sky became a leaden slate, and while the sea turned black, you were too busy to be afraid. You were buffeted by wind blowing thirty-five knots and soaked by rollers breaking over the deck. You concentrated on the emergency of the moment and the Captain's commands as your little craft climbed to the crest of each wave and slid down the trough.

Tonight you fall asleep as your head touches the pillow, immensely proud that when they were needed, your skill counted and your competence made a difference.

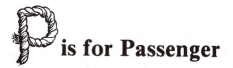 is for Passenger

P is for Passengers. Entertaining on your boat is a little like having a dinner party in your closet. Expect to learn a lot about the hidden side of human nature—the one civilization has covered up—when you take your friends to sea. Some will not remain friends.

Of course, there are those who flatly refuse. They treat your invitation for a day on the boat as if you had invited them to witness an execution. They say, "No, absolutely not, I would never do that."

Having been out once on a small boat, they have promised themselves that as long as they can walk, fight, bite, kick or scream they will not get any closer to the water than the bathtub.

Certainly there are those friends who will become stalwart members of your crew. They heave to, let out the mainsail, duck when the Captain jibes, clean up the potato chips when the Captain jibes, keep quiet when the Captain jibes and take their turn at the helm.

But ChapWoman cautions that there are other kinds of passengers afloat. To be forewarned is to be prepared. All that "Clotheshorse Connie" knows about the sea comes from the spring fashion spread in *Vogue*. She arrives at your humble craft wearing white designer suede pants, a silk shirt, double-breasted blazer with epaulettes and shoes that gouge holes in your gelcoat. And, of course, gold hoop earrings. You wish the sea gulls hadn't beaten her to the boat. After stripping her of her shoes, you spend the rest of the day apologetically wiping the cockpit cushions and pushing her out of the way of the boom.

"Susie Siren" is quite a different story. She wears tight jeans over a string bikini and is wholly responsible for the boat being off course for most of the trip. The Captain can't keep his eyes on the compass. She spends the afternoon

*Chap Woman would like to discuss entertaining on your boat,
which is a little like having a dinner party in your closet.*

sunning, seducing and sipping something cool and frosty which you have prepared in the galley which is anything but cool. You are frosty. She talks a lot about sex. You worry a lot about sex because the only man aboard, other than hers, is yours.

"Reluctant Rachel" is there because her husband made her come. You know she is not happy about the trip when you see her shuffle down the dock dragging her feet, while her husband pushes from behind. Her first statement after her husband shoves her on board is that she can't swim. She wears a life preserver for the next thirty six hours and chains herself to the stanchion by day and the hand rails by night. She says very little. It is a long weekend.

"Cruising Cathy" seems to have confused your invitation with a cruise on the Loveboat. She arrives with two hard-sided suitcases which become weaponry below, changes her clothes several times a day and wonders where she can blow-dry her hair. She definitely expects to have dinner ashore. You take her out to pick crabs in a restaurant, where the tablecloth is a newspaper, and the only implement is a wooden mallet. That's not what she expected.

The men arrive with much more bravado than their mates. A day at sea smacks of Huckleberry Finn, Chichester and Slocum and the threat of pirates. Once on board, they are ready to single-hand around the world. In fact, they are ready to relieve you of command of your ship.

Just take a look at "Helmhog Harry" and "Big Wheel Walt." Harry announces that he has been sailing for years and grabs the tiller the instant his feet leave shore. He does not relinquish it and is oblivious to the Captain's charted course. He follows the wind. Should the Captain take a nap, nobody will know where they are when he awakes. And he will awake quickly because "Helmhog Harry" will either run aground or hit a crab pot. That's when he tells you he can't swim underwater because he has bad ears.

Walt, too, has been waiting to take over the ship. Scratch the surface of Walt and you will find a wild and fearless boy just bursting to get out. He gets out—and on your boat. You wish he hadn't. He hardens up on the sails until you are flattened to the lee side of the boat, listening to five gallons of liquor break loose from their moorings and smash and crash about the cabin sole. With "Big Wheel Walt" at the helm, you look like those pictures in sailing advertisements, except that those people are smiling and laughing, not praying.

"Famished Frank" has no interest in the helm. His fat cells cry out for grub. He will tell you that he doesn't know anything about sailing but he guesses it's okay with him, if you like that sort of thing. He prefers lying on a beach. So he stretches out in the cockpit and eats and drinks: cheese and crackers, coke and beer, sandwiches with three kinds of meat and mustard and mayo, gin and tonics and anything sweet for dessert. By the time you finally get out of the galley and back on deck, he is looking for an afternoon snack and counting the hours until you light the barbeque for dinner. Would you believe that he brought corn-on-the-cob to go with the steak? It takes one and one-half hours to cook corn on the alcohol stove, if you are lucky.

ChapWoman believes that no manual would be complete without mention of "Debby Deep" and husband Dan. For them the only difference between a day on a boat and a day in the therapist's office is that the deck moves. Yes, they are into meaningful relationships, finding themselves, and therapy groups. They go right on discussing whether an affair will strengthen their marriage, while the wind whips up to twenty-five knots and the Captain reefs the main and gets out the safety harnesses. They go on talking while the waves wash over the deck and the Captain tries to take down the jib without being blown overboard. They go below to talk when their sweaters get wet. You hope they get sick.

ChapWoman suggests limiting guests at sea to those you know will heave to, duck and follow commands. When you see the others headed in your direction, quickly decide to spend the day ashore.

 **is for Quarterberth**

Q is for Quarterberth. The quarterberth is billed as an additional sleeping compartment, but ChapWoman knows that you will use it for stowage. It's where you stow the extra sails, the food that doesn't fit anywhere else, the beer, the soft drinks, the towels, the sleeping bags and the toilet paper. Also, the cockpit cushions. Eventually, the mate gets tired of dragging these cushions in and out, every night and morning, and leaves them in the attic back home, year 'round.

The quarterberth is also where you stow the reluctant teen forced to accompany the family on a boating weekend. He lies there like a bear in hibernation, plugged into his Sony Walkman, only emerging from Twisted Sister long enough for meals.

The quarterberth, although the largest storage locker, is not the only one. There are a number of other lockers, which people are usually sitting in front of, or on top of. You wish your guests were 98 pound weaklings, who would be easy to move.

Your mother used to talk about a place for everything and everything in its place. You wonder how she knew so much about boating when she never left Kansas. The trouble with shipboard life is that you must take everything out of its place to get to the place of the item in the back, which is always the item you want.

You keep the big crab pot, which you use three times a year, in the back of the locker behind the port settee. To reach it, you have to remove the sauce pan, the frying pan, the hot plate, the flares, the lanterns and three boxes of cookies and, of course, Uncle Charlie, who weighs two hundred pounds, and is taking a nap on the port settee.

On shipboard, if an object is not stowed behind closed doors, it will either go overboard or become a flying missile

On shipboard, if an object is not stowed behind closed doors, it will either go overboard or become a flying missile below.

below. So when you finish with the pot, you will once again remove Uncle Charlie, who is now sitting with his back comfortably against the port locker. It is his third move. He was sitting on the wine before dinner.

Food is stored in the dry storage locker, a cavern beside the sink which will hold three layers of cans, and is entered from above. When you're putting the provisions away, you don't think about labeling the cans on their ends until you are about to heat up the Dinty Moore Beef Stew while you are underway in a gale. (Boats carry Dinty Moore the way they used to carry hard tack and molasses.) You know that Dinty Moore is in there somewhere, hiding underneath the boxes of milk, the dry cereal, the fruit cocktail, the mayo, catsup, mustard, and the cans of soup. You know it's there but you will have to remove two layers of cans to find it.

Boat designers have provided a dry storage locker and an ice box, but they have not even addressed the problem of produce. The mate must take this into her own hands. You rig hammocks and string bags from the hand rails. You hang bananas, apples, potatoes, onions, peppers and clusters of garlic for the long voyage ahead. The boat has lost its proud, clean lines below and looks a bit like a French peasant's cart on its way to market. In heavy weather, the crew must duck to avoid being beaned by a swinging potato.

ChapWoman recommends stowing at least twenty pounds of potatoes for "navigation by potato" in foggy New England waters. Stand on the bow of the boat and toss a potato. If you don't hear a splash, come about in a big hurry.

Boat designers have allotted you one drawer, a shelf in the vee berth, and the hanging locker for stowage of your clothing. What that really boils down to is the drawer. The shelf in the vee berth will be wet, and the hanging locker will be full of foul weather gear, wind breakers, electrical cord and extra life jackets. You may get away with using the chart table as a *garde-manger* at dinner time, but the Captain will never accept finding your lingerie and blouses beside his dividers and charts. ChapWoman suggests this rule of the sea: if you can't roll it, don't bring it.

Out in the black holes of the cockpit lockers, there are some things that don't fit, so they are sold cut in half, like the oars and the fishing rods; some things that won't come out once they go in, like the sail bag and the inflatable dinghy and occasionally the Captain; and, of course, some things that are more trouble to remove than they're worth. For instance, the hose. Use the hose that is already on the dock, whenever possible.

Speaking of trouble, let's get back to the Captain, who's still in the lazerette. He claims he climbed in there to check the steering cable. Now, like Winnie the Pooh, he finds it harder to exit than it was to enter the hole's opening. You wonder about having him laid out in the lazerette and how you'd handle the crowd.

Yes, stowage is a problem. You carry a reasonable number of things to the boat in the spring. You place them carefully in the lockers, lazerette, shelves and drawers. They lie there all summer in the moist darkness and multiply. Like the miracle of the loaves and fishes, it takes three station wagon runs to decommission your vessel in the fall.

 **is for Raft Up**

R is for Raft-Up. The raft-up is the oasis at the end of the mate's day, the icing on her cake. Sometimes, it is a relief from the twosome that makes you wonder about the "as long as you both shall live" part of the marriage ceremony.

All sorts of days at sea end in a raft with congenial sailors. On a rough day, you will sail twenty-seven miles on your side, hoping that you will live long enough to anchor, raft-up and discover horizontal again. On a stifling day, you motor for six hours in a heat haze, hoping that you'll survive to anchor, raft-up and plunge into some cool, clear water and into a lot of cool, clear gin. On an ideal day, the wind is fresh, the sails are full. You arrive at your anchorage at sunset, eager to raft with fellow rovers and swap tales about the day's adventures.

Your friends are already there when you arrive. You get out bumpers. They get out bumpers. You turn your attention to tossing lines back and forth and trussing up your two boats like a Thanksgiving turkey. No pleasantries are exchanged during this tense time. The guests, who are sailing with you, think you are incredibly rude. No introductions are made, although there are six or eight people standing eyeball to eyeball. No one shakes hands across the lifeline or says, "How was your sail?"

Instead, you throw out your bow line and then your stern line and keep your mast and stern aft of the other boat so that you don't lock spreaders in the night. You attach the forward quarter spring from their bow to your stern to keep from sliding backward; you attach the after spring from their stern to your bow to keep from sliding forward. The mates scurry around weaving the boats together while the Captains stand at the helm, giving orders. Both Captains shout that the bumpers are in the wrong place. Trying to push two seven-ton boats apart while moving a bumper fore or aft, is like holding up a car while somebody changes a

Charcoal fires glow on the sterns. The aroma of barbecued chicken mixes with steak as the moon rises and sailors on one boat start singing old college songs.

tire. ChapWoman says that if you like your lifelines taut, don't use them to push the boats apart. Use the shrouds.

Sometimes in large raft-ups, due to the grim determination required for the job and the fact that, at the end of the day most boaters are weary and most boats look alike, you may glance up from cleating and trussing and squeezing bumpers to discover that you are tied to a total stranger. It's one of the hazards of boating.

But once secured, you think you have died and gone to heaven. Green lawns slope down to the shore, the bluefish and bass leap, water spiders skate by in pairs, and a shy, long-legged heron stands by the bank with his hands in his pockets. You curl up in your neighbor's cockpit and watch the shadows lengthen on a bay that looks like a piece of velvet brushed here and there the wrong way. On the far bank, cattails, like frankfurters, are roasting against the sunset's fire.

Somewhere on shore, you hear the noises of a telephone ringing, voices calling, a car starting. You are glad that you are out here where nobody can find you.

Rafts in an anchorage are like hometown stoops on a Saturday night. You visit back and forth and dink over to other boats. Charcoal fires glow on the sterns. The aroma of barbecued chicken mixes with steak as the moon rises and sailors on one boat start singing old college songs. The twinkling stars lean close and a few lose their hold and fall through the infinite, black vastness of the night.

The ambience of a raft-up is so nurturing that you drift off to sleep, lulled by the cricket chorus on the shore. When you wake the next morning, the sky is blue, and the breeze fresh. You join the boats setting sail and plan another raft-up thirty miles down the bay. You'll swim and read and visit and tell sea stories all over again tonight.

Back home, trapped in the routine of ringing telephones, carpools and grocery shopping, you'll dream of rafting-up, eating topside, watching the sun set and the moon rise. You long to repeat those magical moments when you feel young and free, unfettered by cares, worries and responsibilities.

 **S is for Skipper**

S is for Skipper. ChapWoman understands that when boating first becomes part of a Skipper's life, a dutiful mate, glad to be of help in this new adventure, will willingly lend a hand.

However, be prepared for a character change in the Skipper. There is something about stepping aboard his own boat, small as that may be, that brings out the Captain Bligh in the mildest of men.

When the Skipper barks: "Break out the genoa, tighten up the main halyard and be prepared to jibe" . . . it is not considered proper for you to reply "You're kidding!" There is a basic, universal law that ChapWoman urges you to remember: "put a man on a boat and he starts giving orders to the crew". And you know who that is, don't you?

At times, it will be hard to believe that the lunatic straddling the tiller, yelling into the wind with all the gusto that he's got, his hair streaming out behind him, is the one you took for better or worse. Only yesterday, he appeared perfectly normal, standing on the station platform in coat and tie, waiting for the 8:02.

You simply cannot believe that your shy, mild-mannered homebody has started glancing around with a roguish expression. There's a devilish gleam in the look he gives the pretty, young things lolling about him. He prowls the deck, at the ready to attack a luff, tighten a sheet, adjust a traveler. He handles his winches a lot. He seems distracted and bemused. He murmurs sweet nothings in his sleep. He says this time he wants a trim one. You look in the mirror. You are no longer trim. He doesn't mean you. Can it be, after all these years, that your Skipper is acquiring a roving eye?

ChapWoman offers this guidance for making the best of a trying time. Remember that it all began with the Skipper behaving like a typical male, surrounded by a bevy of well-

There is something about stepping aboard his own boat, that brings out the Captain Bligh in the mildest of men.

built, frisky playthings who invite his attention and admiration. Few ardent sailors are interested in much beyond outward appearance and performance.

Even though the older, gentle, round bottomed tub may be more suitable for the wear and tear of the long voyage, you can bet your bell-rope that it's the sleek, trim-lined model that catches the male eye and billfold.

You know her type. Superbly outfitted, she glides smoothly along, making no waves; at all times, aloof, serene and terribly expensive. The Skipper goes crazy. Often, on getting better acquainted, he finds that there is much less to her than first met the eye.

Women understand these things instinctively and are patient with their Skippers. Nine times out of ten, the boat finally chosen, although not exactly virginal, having been badly neglected by her previous owners, is one whose beauty shines through her peeling paint. Her pride of bearing is regal beneath her tattered rags. She has character. So do you. The Skipper *is* one.

Bringing her into the family requires many hours of joint labor. You have to work at the relationship. Her new outfit of sails makes your longed-for mink coat look cheap by comparison. Also out of the question.

But, as you chip her paint, sand her bottom and scrub her teak, you know that although she will never match your nobility of spirit, she is shaping up quite well.

When the last sliver of teak has been oiled, the final blister patched, and her bottom painted a becoming blue, the Skipper grins. He is satisfied—jubilant even.

You are grinning too. You have made peace with your rival. In fact, you have accomplished the impossible. Believe it or not, you find that you have actually been able to accept and even enjoy your own ménage à trois.

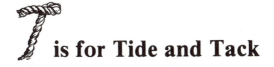 is for **Tide and Tack**

ChapWoman defines Tide as the movement of water in which your boat is sitting. The movement may be up and down (tidal range); or it may be back and forth (tidal current). When you are dealing with water, remember that something is happening with it all the time. Like a two year old, water is never still and bears careful watching.

Sailors spend many hours talking about tide and current. They buy books with lots of tables in them. These are officially called Daily Tide Predictions but the mate knows better. They are the Captain's *Racing Form*. He's going to use the information to try to figure the odds, think about his track, and wonder about the weather conditions. Dealing with tide and current is always a gamble. When the Captain says there will be lots of water under the boat at low tide, ChapWoman says: "Don't put your money on it."

Anchoring for the night will certainly present difficulties if your calculations concerning tidal range are inaccurate. The vessel that floats gently at high tide in the evening, may lie on its side like a sick sea lion at low tide next morning. You become aware of this happening when you fall out of your berth at dawn. The next surprise awaiting you is the fact that the head is out of commission until the next high tide. Given a fifty-fifty chance, your boat will certainly choose to roll over onto the side where the head is not.

Short cuts across bars and reefs may produce still another surprise, coupled with grief. If the Captain's interpolations of the heights above or below the datum level have been affected by such things as the diurnal inequality at quadrature, then you're in trouble. Sailors really do like to run off at the mouth once they start in about the moon's gravitational pull.

When about to cross a bar or a reef, ask the Captain if, in his calculations, he remembered to add an hour for daylight-saving time. If you ask before the reef, it will show

When about to cross a bar or a reef, ask the Captain if, in his calculations, he remembered to add an hour for daylight-saving time.

him that you are paying attention. Once you are mired in sand and sludge, it may get you a fat lip.

T is also for Tack. The dictionary defines tack as a zigzag course of action, sharply divergent from that previously followed; or a sticky condition. ChapWoman says: "Right on."

It is important to know which tack you are on, because that determines who has the right of way. But, as in all things nautical, don't expect this to be easy to figure out.

The tack is determined by which side the wind is blowing from, and the easiest way to decide this, is to realize it's the side the sail is not on. Of course, we're talking mainsail here, the other sails can be anywhere they feel like being. So, if your mainsail is on the port side, that means you are on a starboard tack and have the right of way. That is, unless the boat about to cross (or perhaps splinter) your bow is also on a starboard tack. Then it's the leeward boat which gets to go first. This brings us back to our original definition of tack as a zigzag course and a sticky condition.

The time to tack usually occurs whenever the mate has just stretched out comfortably in the shade with a good book. Himself waits until you turn a page, with a contented sigh. The heroine has told her lover that she is pregnant and he has told his wife, who has suggested that she come live with them until the baby is born. This is the moment that the Captain announces "Ready About."

A dutiful mate rises to the occasion. She puts down her book, grasps the jib-sheet, checks for the winch handle and says, "Ready." The next few seconds require her to possess the grace and agility of Mikhail Baryshnikov and the strength and muscular coordination of Arnold Schwarzenegger. When the Captain shouts "Hard Alee," she must release the jib carefully, grasp the other sheet, wrap it around the winch, drop the winch handle in place and winch in the genoa, while the boat tilts like a see-saw.

Actually, you can forget that part about grace and agility. To be perfectly frank, the most important requirement needed for this job is the brute strength of a gorilla. It is the reason why people who do it on the Newport to Bermuda races are called "Deck Apes." It is also why there are often bunches of bananas hanging from the rigging of racing vessels.

Tacking is the procedure that a boat goes through whenever its destination is the place where the wind is coming from. ChapWoman has noticed this is practically always.

 # U is for Uniform

U is for Uniform. It is desirable for the Captain and the crew to maintain a certain degree of jaunty, nautical nattiness of dress and manner aboard ship.

There are some sailors (though certainly not on *your* vessel), who seem to have an innate sense of nautical fashion. They combine easy, casual good looks with traditional, classic born-to-yachting style. They are the ones aboard the Race Committee Boat who wear the Yacht Club necktie with their swim trunks and nothing else, and manage to look great doing it. Besides a marvelous tan, they always have exquisite, white teeth.

Their mates match them in perfection. Nothing wrinkles, wilts or sags. This applies to their clothing, skin, and hair. Even their fingernails are in tact after a day of hoisting, hauling and sail handling. They slip easily from color-coordinated tops and shorts, to delightful swim-togs, to charming blouses and wrap skirts for evening. They have figures to which their clothes cling in admiration. They are enough to make you want to puke.

Aboard your boat, however, the Captain is one who glories in being called "a rag man" and dresses to fit the part. He is the one who wears a three-day growth of beard, a Fruit-of-the-Loom label showing above his pants and dirty sneakers. His uniform of the day is pants that are patched with flesh. His goal apparently, is to resemble as closely as possible, Humphrey Bogart in *"The African Queen."* Of course, you pack his alligator shirt and pants. Then he wears them when he takes the engine apart on Saturday morning. Although he denies it, the holes in his clothes bear out your suspicions that he dabs battery acid on himself as though it were eau de cologne.

On your boat, sad to say, you understand the meaning of the term "motley crew." It's not that you don't try. It's just

*There are some sailors (though certainly not on **your** vessel), who seem to have an innate sense of nautical fashion.*

that you weren't born with naturally curly hair. It's that the years of sun and sea have etched the lines deeper; the hard tack and molasses have made the curves rounder and fuller; the anxiety and worry have erased the joie de vivre that those mates who are younger and less sea-wise exhibit.

However, with thought and practice, the mate may compensate for what she lacks in nautical fashion by becoming adept in nautical etiquette. ChapWoman says that a certain code of manners still applies aboard ship.

1) Just as a good soldier never looks back, so a good sailor never looks below. The understanding hostess always stands in the cockpit with her back to the companion-way, blocking the view, so that a guest may slip in and out of a bathing suit with propriety.

2) Never peek through port holes. When four to six people are spending a week together in an area of 36 by 10 feet, it's like playing the childhood game "Sardines in a Can." Any semblance of privacy is jealously guarded.

3) Conserve water at all times. This means turn off the faucet while brushing your teeth, running water only to rinse your toothbrush. This may sound picky, but rest assured, that no matter where he is on the boat, the Captain is listening in horror as the water pump pulsates.

4) The same goes for battery power. The Captain's blood pressure climbs in direct proportion to the wattage being used. Keep your Captain happy. Turn off the light you don't need.

5) Don't climb on another vessel without having been invited aboard first. There are those who feel it is permissible to hail the Captain or even rap discreetly on the hull. ChapWoman says: Never. Remember it's possible that all hands have already seen you coming and are hiding out below.

 **is for Varnish**

V is for Varnish which is one of the many things that people put on their teak. Before buying a boat, you probably didn't know much about teak or that you and your spouse would spend so much of your remaining life discussing it. Back then, you played golf and tennis and read books. Now you talk teak, think teak, oil teak, scrub teak and varnish teak.

Your teak will need all the attention it gets because teak does not age gracefully. It ages immediately. The smooth, plump, honey-colored hand rail that you bought in April will be wrinkled and grooved, blackened in places, withered and grey by September.

Which is why at parties you'll hear the man in your life say, "What do you put on your teak?" right after he says "Hello." He will debate in depth the merits of oils and varnishes with bank presidents, lawyers and eastern shore crabbers. The state of the world, the IRS and what's wrong with the NFL take a back seat to a heated discussion of Teak Brite®, Teak Wonder®, Tip Top Teak®, Deks Olje® and Semco® — the golden or the natural and maybe mixing the two—and of course, varnish, which he thinks makes a boat look pockmarked by fall.

Yes, men feel deeply about their teak, which brings us to one of the most bizarre facts of boating. Men not only do housework at sea, but talk about it, too. At home, in his house or his condo, the man in your life does not hang over the back fence discussing Ajax, Comet and Janitor in A Drum. He doesn't polish furniture or mop the kitchen floor. You do it, or if you go on strike, you pay a cleaning woman to do it.

But on the boat he wields a broom and a deck mop and has orgies with suds. He even asks your marina mate what he puts in his bucket. You can't believe it. The man with the

Which is why at parties, you'll hear the man in your life say, "What do you put on your teak?" right after he says "hello."

briefcase, the horn-rimmed glasses, and the office on the twentieth floor with a secretary who still brings him coffee, is talking detergent power and loving it.

He cleans the cockpit and the chrome, coils the line and, smart man that he is, he only talks about the teak. One of the reasons you do your own teak is that you couldn't afford to pay someone to do it for you. It takes less time to clean a four bedroom house, iron seven shirts, fix lunch and dinner for the kids, clean the cellar and the oven, than it does to do the teak. That's because you don't have to be a contortionist to do the house.

The job wouldn't be so bad if you had lots of nice flat slabs of teak all over the place that you could rub down like a horse. Instead, you have curved pieces and spindly pieces, rolled-over pieces and long, skinny pieces on the wrong side of the life-line.

There are teak toe rails, teak hand holds to the companionway, teak grates in the floor, teak racks for glasses and—the crowning blow—whole decks made of teak. Don't let us forget the teak steps on the swim ladder. To do these you must hang over the stern like a possum, clutching the ladder in one hand, a can in the other, and the scrub brush between your teeth. The water is forty degrees and you wish you knew more about hypothermia and whether the Captain, who has his head in the engine, will hear you if you fall in. And if he does hear you, will he do anything about it?

Men always do the engines while the women do the teak, although men talk a lot about how to do the teak. Some believe in sanding it and others in scrubbing it, but no matter which way you go, doing the teak is not a pleasant job.

You crouch inside the lifeline, you crouch outside the lifeline, you huddle on the dog house and squat on the bow, you hunch and you bend double. Finally, the teak is done. The grooves, the grey color and the black lines are gone and once again the teak is young, smooth and a pale golden color. You wish you were, too.

Your Captain caresses the hand rail and runs his fingers over the toe rail and approves the job. He is ready to discuss the stain.

Now don't be surprised that he's so deeply committed to the color of his teak, even though he still hasn't noticed that you redecorated the living room a year ago. No man will ever feel the same about his home as he does about his boat.

Once he decides on the stain, you will go through the whole teak procedure again. You will crouch and hunch and squat. But now you are squatting, hunching and crouching with a rag and a cup of stain and you are also listening to the Captain sound off about not spilling on the gelcoat.

Over the years, the murmur of distress of wives doing teak has turned into a steady roar, finally heard by boat designers in northern climes. In Canada they are building their boats like their cars, using stainless steel instead of teak.

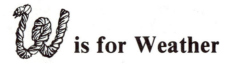 **is for Weather**

W is for Weather. When the wind's up on the "Ideal Day," time rarely hangs heavy on a sailboat. The Captain sees to it that all hands are busy. He's in his glory and you truly enjoy watching his soul stretching itself in the freshening breeze. He says this is what sailing is all about. You are caught up in the spirit. You see clipper ship clouds in a sky so blue you wish you could wear it. You remember Bing Crosby and Grace Kelly singing "True Love" and calling their boat "yar." You recall lines about "flung spray and blown spume."

So you hoist and winch and take the helm and play boat with him. You watch your mahogany-faced Captain standing erect and proud, pleased with himself and his surroundings. You are glad to be part of this, since it makes him so happy. Today that is enough. It won't be under other conditions.

Treasure every moment of the Ideal Day and when you lose it, try to remember what it was like. Particularly on the "Rough Day."

At least you won't be bored on the Rough Day. Sheer terror keeps you on your toes. Rough weather is a nautical euphemism for anything from a line squall to force twelve winds in a hurricane. You can expect to be out in it because men of the sea seem to think that they look much better bundled up in foul weather gear, braving the elements.

The same thunder shower which makes you get up and close a few windows at home, will, on a boat, convince you that Mother Nature woke up this morning with a crackerjack case of P.M.S. When a big whiff of ozone clears your sinuses, and a bolt of lightening turns the air blue, there's nothing like a tall, metal mast standing alone in a large body of water to remind you of your own mortality. You think about why sea captains and airline pilots refer to their passengers as "souls". On rough days you will do a lot of thinking about the meaning of life.

ChapWoman has done some research on how those familiar with the sea deal with rough weather. Some subdivisions on the section from boating manuals are: Beam seas. Running inlets. Stranding and towing. Man overboard. Leaks and damage control. Abandoning ship. Helicopter rescue. Can you believe it, helicopter rescue? Even ChapWoman hadn't thought of that one! . . . kind of makes you think twice, doesn't it? The list sounds like a litany to which the reply would be "Deliver us, O Lord."

You certainly hope prayer works on the "Foggy Day". One Sunday morning you will awaken in your snug, out-of-the-way anchorage and discover that overnight the fog has crept in on little cat feet. The view from the porthole reminds you of the movie "Sands of Iwo Jima" or the fumaroles in Yellowstone. Eddies of mist rise from the water, veiling everything in a dull sallow light. You know, however, that John Wayne will not appear, nor are you safe on land in Wyoming. You are two shipping channels away from your home port.

The morning progresses. The fog wraps even tighter. Captain Vigilant gets antsy. He wants to put the show on the road. Actually, you could get home faster by crawling on your hands and knees, since there is no wind. You motor cautiously, turning off the engine every few mintues to listen for what is moving around out there. When motoring, you give periodic blasts on your air horn.

When stopped, you ring the ship's bell. Locating the bell involves a lengthy exchange between the Captain and the mate over who stowed the bell where, when. The ship's bell, like the last remaining beer on board, vanishes without a trace on foggy Sunday afternoons.

The Captain hoists the radar reflector up the mast. The tiny contraption that looks like a sand-toy, has already disappeared into the swirling mist twenty feet above your head. It is all that stands between you and certain destruction. The Captain expects you to believe that it will make big, bright blips on the radar screens of the freighers, tankers and steamers cruising the shipping channel. You

The fog has crept in on little cat feet.

don't believe in the Sugar Plum Fairy and you don't put much credence in the radar, either.

You toot, ring, blip and grope your way to port. Once again, you cheat death. The awesome weight of worrying your boat home in the fog has exhausted you. Just as you secure the last line, the sun appears in all its glory. The fog begins to lift.

Treasure every return to port. You are now entitled to utter those immortal words coined by sailors' mates in centuries past: "Down the Hatch."

Xray, Yankee, Zulu

XYZ is for Xray, Yankee, Zulu. In other words, the VHF Marine radiotelephone. ChapWoman knows that a woman is never at ease without a telephone handy. It's not that she wants to use it all the time. It's just that she feels safer and more confident knowing that it is there. With a cup of coffee in one hand and the telephone in the other, most women find that they can handle the vicissitudes of life with equanimity. This is especially true on a boat.

Right after you learn to light the alcohol stove, make the mastery of the VHF marine radio your next project. Most of the time your marine radio will be set on Channel 16. What you hear when you listen sounds like the construction

The "Fishing Fibbers" call the little woman to report the whole bay is socked in with fog and they can't get home till Sunday night. There isn't a cloud in the sky.

gang at work on the Tower of Babel. There's a lot of name calling. Everyone talks. Nobody listens.

The first step is to wait for a break in the stream of voices. Your roots will grow out while you do. But you'll gain valuable insights into the human race. Nowhere will you discover a better method of discerning the character of people whom you have never met, than by using the VHF or radio telephone—often called the "soap of the sea."

There are the "Radio Hogs." They monopolize the channel chatting about the anchorage, the race, and who has the beer, until the Coast Guard tells them to get off. You're glad that they identified their boat so you can avoid them in an anchorage.

The "Poor Lonely Souls" need a radio check. They call the Coast Guard. They call anybody at all out there within range of their voice. They continue to call for a radio check after six boats have answered to assure them that they are coming through loud and clear. You feel sorry for them because they don't ever seem to know anybody who boats. You devoutly wish they'd find some other lonely radio checker, strike up a friendship, and get off the airways.

The "Impossible Dreamers" entreat and implore bridge tenders, harbor masters and the mechanic at the yacht charter office to answer them on the VHF. Everybody knows that bridge tenders, harbor masters and mechanics are not sitting around monitoring Channel 16. They are either down the street having a beer, closed for the day, out of business or listening to another channel.

So much for the radio freaks. All that the telephoners want to do is call home. The "Fishing Fibbers" are down on the boat with a bunch of guys having a blast. They call the little woman to report that the whole bay is socked in with fog and they can't get home till Sunday night. Their position is three miles from yours. There isn't a cloud in the sky.

The "Compulsive Moms" call home Friday night. They left that afternoon at 3:30, but by Friday night they are on the line checking out the history assignment and the kids' baseball game, inning by inning. Meanwhile, the marine operator has the calls in a holding pattern like JFK on Christmas Eve.

The "Naughtie Nellies" steam up the airways after midnight and account for the X in the XYZ.

ChapWoman has noticed that spending half an hour minding other peoples' business on the VHF can spice up a long day's cruising and is better than *"All My Children"* and *"General Hospital."*

Just about the time you think you have become an extension of the quarterberth cushion and that the foam has entered your soul, there will be a break in the radio chatter. Jump right in and recite the name of the boat you are calling three times, then the name of your vessel and its call letters. Try to cultivate friends who select simple, no-nonsense names for their boats. "Sorceress' Song" may look nice on the transom but trying saying it rapidly three times.

Once you have established contact, switch to your working channel. Talk for less than three minutes, give your boat name and call letters and sign out. Anybody who can accomplish this feat without being unacknowledged, interrupted, stepped on, or garbled should send their name and address to the *Guiness Book of Records.*

When you finally do make contact and switch to the working channel, the first question asked you will be: Where are you? Be assured that wherever you were when you went below to call is certainly not where you are now. ChapWoman suggests selecting a few buoys or landmarks along the day's course and jotting down their coordinates. Stay off the radio until you see them on the horizon. You will astound your shipmates, and the whole conglomeration of eavesdroppers waiting for you to get off the horn, when you give them a snappy: "Our location is approximately Latitude: 39 degrees, 12 minutes 30 seconds North; Longitude: 76 degrees 21 minutes 4 seconds West." That ought to get you a few minutes of awed silence even from the Captain. Moments like this can make a mate's day.

The time to get the hang of the VHF is on those days when you don't need it, when the bay is buttered over with calm and the boats trail long wakes of watered silk.

On rough, stormy days, when a freighter is coming right at you, you want to be able to introduce yourself pleasantly to the freighter captain, mention politely to him that you are down there below him, hidden in a trough and doing your best to get out of his way. You want to ask him if he would mind telling you where he is planning to go next. When he finally comes on the radio, you realize that all your efforts at radio communication have been in vain. You don't speak Japanese.

Nautical Maxims

A bolt in the hand is worth two in the bilge.

The time to reef is usually half an hour ago.

Tomorrow's destination is always directly up wind.

Now that you've gone to fibreglass, beware of polyestermites.

If you don't know where you are, the next buoy is no help.

The smoothness of your docking varies inversely with the number of people standing on the dock.

Rings arounds the moon presage rain; rings around two moons presage a bad hangover.

Life is like a rowboat; we cannot move ahead without looking backward.

Emergency lines are pieces of rope too good to throw out.

Many hands make a crowded boat.

The old oaken bucket needs no holding tank.

Pouring oil on troubled waters is a violation of federal law.

When your draft exceeds your depth, you are aground.

A Rhodes by any other name would sail as sweet . . .

A collision at sea can ruin your whole day.

Coriolis was a cross-eyed nymph in Greek mythology.

A spinnaker makes a wonderful sea anchor.

Anyone can hold the helm when the sea is calm.

Nature loves the hidden flaw.

Measure twice, cut once.

CAN YOU IDENTIFY THESE NAUTICAL CHARACTERS? They are found in the Bible, in Novels, Poems, Nursery Rhymes, and the Comics

1. A powerful, green-vegetable lover.
2. A pretty-boy and snappy-dresser who may be sued for breach-of-promise.
3. Drunken skipper gets steamed up over prissy, psalm-singing old maid.
4. Villain, bothered by a tick, pursued by a reptile.
5. Amorous, feathered musician travels with catty paramour in well-provisioned vessel.
6. He stuck to deep water but touched bottom anyway.
7. Peg-legged villain and sometime cook.
8. This adventurer stole a ride on a bird.
9. One track mind and a one legged body, his quarry found him.
10. Subject of a miraculous man-overboard drill.
11. Boat builder and first recorded zoo-keeper.
12. Skillful tactician in naval battles, but so shy around women that he didn't live up to his name.
13. Got his comeuppance for taking his cruelty out on a Christian.
14. Unable captain whose crew raises cain.
15. A bore at weddings, who learned his lesson by having more than a ring around his collar.
16. A strong swimmer undone by hero-worship.
17. A bureaucrat who cornered the market in brass-polish.
18. Traveler and irrascible host who spun an epic yarn explaining a 10-year absence to his long suffering wife.

Nautical Characters Answers

1. Popeye
2. Bobbie Shaftoe
3. Charlie Alnutt — African Queen
4. Captain Hook
5. Owl in "The Owl and the Pussycat"
6. Captain Nemo
7. Long John Silver
8. Sinbad
9. Captain Ahab
10. Jonah
11. Noah
12. Horatio Hornblower
13. Captain Bligh
14. Captain Queeg
15. Ancient Mariner
16. Leander
17. Sir Joseph Porter (Pinafore)
18. Ulysses